Anne Hutchinson

Struggle for Religious Freedom

Bruce T. Paddock

Boston, Massachusetts
Chandler, Arizona
Glenview, Illinois
Upper Saddle River, New Jersey

Illustrations
Opener, 1, 2, 3, 5, 7, 8, 9, 10, 12, 13, 14, 15 Wes Lowe.

Photographs
Every effort has been made to secure permission and provide appropriate credit for photographic material. The publisher deeply regrets any omission and pledges to correct errors called to its attention in subsequent editions.

Unless otherwise acknowledged, all photographs are the property of Pearson Education, Inc.

Photo locators denoted as follows: Top (T), Center (C), Bottom (B), Left (L), Right (R), Background (Bkgd)

All Photos: Library of Congress.

ISBN-13: 978-0-328-67690-3
ISBN-10: 0-328-67690-X

5 6 V0FL 16 15 14 13

Who Was Anne Hutchinson?

As a young girl, Anne Marbury was given an excellent education by her father.

Anne Hutchinson and her family came to the Massachusetts Bay Colony in 1634 so that they could practice their religion freely. Hutchinson was well educated and had strong opinions about religion. But in Massachusetts Bay Colony, a woman could get in trouble for voicing her opinions. And that is just what happened. The storm Hutchinson created threatened the Massachusetts Bay Colony, but it helped plant the seed for the idea of religious freedom that would later grow in our country.

Anne Marbury was born in England in 1591. Her father was a minister in the Anglican Church. He got in trouble for criticizing the way Anglican **officials** ran the church.

Reverend Marbury taught his children at home. Anne Marbury was very smart, and studied hard. Her father taught her to think for herself and to stand up for her opinions. Her mother taught her to be a midwife, someone trained to help deliver babies.

In 1612, Anne Marbury married William Hutchinson. William made a good living as a merchant, buying and selling goods. Together, they had 15 children.

Over time, Anne Hutchinson's ideas about religion changed. She became a Puritan. Puritans believed that the Anglican Church needed to be purified, or stripped of its bad practices. Anglican Church officials spoke out against Puritans and even **persecuted** them. So, in 1634, Hutchinson and her family moved to Boston.

In the 1600s, many Puritans fled England for Massachusetts.

The Massachusetts Bay Colony

The Massachusetts Bay Colony had been established in 1630 by a group of Puritans seeking religious freedom—for themselves, at least. They were led by John Winthrop, who was elected the colony's first governor. Winthrop wanted the settlement to be "a city on a hill" and serve as an example for all the world to see.

The colony was based on the Puritan religion and the Bible. Building the colony in the wilderness was hard work. Everyone had to work hard and do what they were supposed to do. If they did, the Puritans were sure that God would bless them and the colony would succeed.

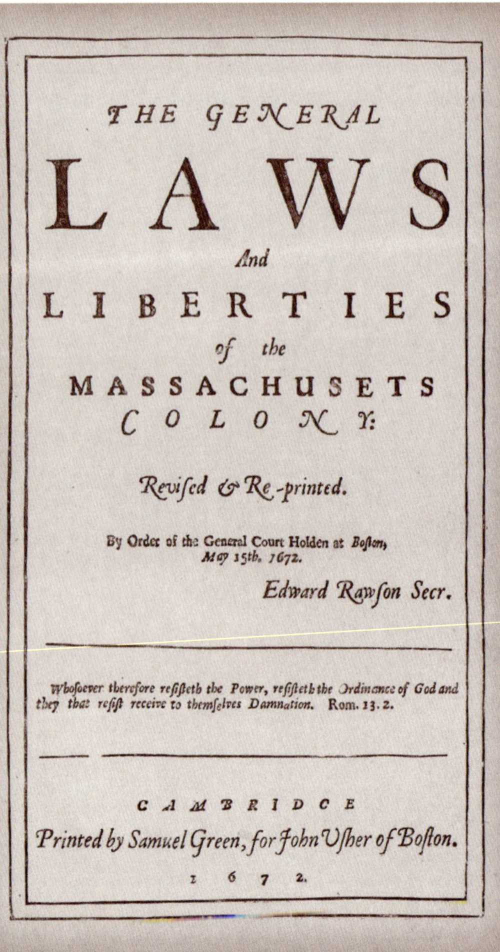

THE GENERAL

LAWS

And

LIBERTIES

of the

MASSACHUSETS

COLONY:

Revised & Re-printed.

By Order of the General Court Holden at *Boston*, *May* 15th. 1672.

Edward Rawson Secr.

Whosoever therefore resisteth the Power, resisteth the Ordinance of God and they that resist receive to themselves Damnation. Rom. 13. 2.

CAMBRIDGE

Printed by Samuel Green, for John Usher of Boston.

1672.

Laws in the Massachusetts Bay Colony were based on the Bible. Each male member of the colony signed an agreement to live by the church's rules.

Governor Winthrop lived in a large, comfortable house like this one. It was just opposite the Hutchinsons' house.

The Hutchinsons

Anne Hutchinson and her husband were well respected in the colony. Will Hutchinson was a successful merchant, and Anne Hutchinson was a skilled midwife. A midwife was important to the community. The couple had a happy marriage and many children. To the Puritans, this was a sign that God blessed them.

It was a custom in the community for women to meet in each others' homes to discuss the week's Bible readings and the sermons. Soon Hutchinson was holding meetings in her home. Hutchinson was a **devout** Puritan and a good speaker. She knew the Bible well. Her meetings became more and more popular.

Henry Vane was an early supporter of Anne Hutchinson.

Hutchinson's Meetings

Many people were coming to Anne Hutchinson's meetings. Men began to attend, too. Important people began attending, including a number of government officials. One of these officials was the colony's governor, Henry Vane.

Henry Vane was a young man who boarded at the home of Anne Hutchinson's minister, Reverend John Cotton. He came from an important family in England. Henry Vane was a newcomer to the colony, but John Winthrop lost the election for governor to him in 1636.

At first the people at the meetings just discussed the week's sermons. But soon Hutchinson began to share her own beliefs. She said that true godliness, or goodness, came from an inner experience of God. Without that, people would not go to heaven. People could not earn their own way to heaven, no matter how closely they followed the Puritan leaders' laws and teachings. There was nothing wrong with this. This was the teaching that the Puritan religion was based on.

But according to Hutchinson, only two Boston ministers really understood the Bible and were teaching correctly. One of these was her minister, John Cotton. She went on to explain exactly why Cotton was correct in his understanding and the other ministers were not.

Both men and women came to listen to Anne Hutchinson interpret the ministers' sermons.

Trouble in the Colony

Hutchinson was headed for trouble. She said that most of the ministers were teaching the wrong ideas. What was worse, she doubted that the other ministers had ever had a real inner experience of God. She even doubted that they would go to heaven! The church and the government were closely connected. By criticizing the minsters, Hutchinson was attacking the colony itself. Before long, Anne Hutchinson's meetings were dividing the colony. Neither the ministers nor the government officials could allow this to happen. If they did, the colony could be destroyed.

There was another reason Anne Hutchinson could get in trouble. She was a woman. In Puritan **society**, women were not supposed to challenge men. They were not supposed to criticize them or tell them what to do. They were not supposed to teach men anything.

In Puritan society, women could be full church members, but they were not allowed to take an active part in services.

So in October of 1636, the ministers held a meeting of their own. They questioned Hutchinson, her brother-in-law Reverend John Wheelwright, and Reverend Cotton. Wheelwright and Cotton talked to the others and convinced them that they all believed and preached the same things. Everyone let the matter rest for the moment.

John Cotton had been the Hutchinsons' minister in England.

Meanwhile, Hutchinson continued holding her meetings. She was certain she was doing what God wanted her to do. Besides, Governor Vane was a friend of hers. But the situation was about to change.

In May of 1637, elections were held. Henry Vane was voted out of office, and John Winthrop was governor again. Winthrop had long been opposed to Hutchinson. He did not like the things she said and did. And Hutchinson was destroying the unity of Winthrop's "city on a hill." She was tearing apart the colony! Winthrop could not allow that.

In August of 1637, the ministers met again. They made a list of 82 religious statements Hutchinson had made that they said were incorrect. Then they arrested several of Hutchinson's followers. All of them were tried and found guilty. Finally, the ministers turned their attention to Hutchinson herself.

Anne Hutchinson defended herself against her accusers.

Hutchinson on Trial

In the trials you might see on television today, each side is represented by a lawyer. Trials in the colony were different. As the **defendant**, the person on trial, Hutchinson had no one to represent her. On the other side of the courtroom, 49 church and government officials sat ready to accuse her. Her main accuser was Governor Winthrop himself, who ran the trial.

Winthrop was not sure how to charge her. In his opening remarks Winthrop told Hutchinson that her meetings were "not tolerable nor comely [proper] in the sight of God." He threatened that if she continued to be stubborn, the court would take action against her.

Hutchinson was not frightened. She responded that she had not yet heard any charges.

Winthrop knew she had not done anything criminal. Still, he called on witnesses, including ministers, who said that Hutchinson had accused them of preaching the wrong ideas.

Hutchinson was smarter than most of her accusers. She denied their claims, and she answered their questions skillfully. At one point, Winthrop asked her why she held meetings on the same evening every week.

"It is lawful for me to do so," Hutchinson replied. She added that others held weekly meetings as well, so why did they blame her for doing the same thing? She also pointed out that it was a custom for women to meet. She was not the first to do it.

John Winthrop was elected governor of the Massachusetts Bay Colony 12 times. Elections in the colony were held every year.

Anne Hutchinson's punishment could have been worse. Mary Dyer, one of Hutchinson's followers, was sentenced to death for her religious beliefs in 1660.

Anne Hutchinson's quick answers annoyed her accusers. They were waiting for her to stumble, and on the second day of the trial, she did. She was asked how she knew that the ministers' teachings were wrong. She replied that God had spoken to her and told her what was true. Then she went on to say that if the ministers continued the way they were going, teaching incorrectly, they would bring down God's punishment on themselves.

The governor could take no more. With a show of hands, the court officials voted on her guilt. Governor Winthrop delivered the verdict:

"Mrs. Hutchinson, the sentence of the court you hear is that you are **banished** . . . as being a woman not fit for our society." Anne Hutchinson would have to leave the colony forever.

On to Rhode Island

On a spring day in 1638, Hutchinson, her family, and about 60 of her followers left Boston. They traveled to Providence, a colony founded two years earlier by Roger Williams. He had also been banished from Boston for his religious teachings.

Some of the group bought a nearby island from the Narragansett, the Native Americans who lived there. The island was called Aquidneck. They started a settlement on the northern part of the island. Anne Hutchinson was one of its founders, but as a woman, she could not be a leader. Legally, John Clark and William Coddington were the first leaders. The settlement was called by its Narragansett name, Pocasett. Today it is Portsmouth, Rhode Island.

New England Colonies, 1638

Hutchinson and her followers left Boston and moved to what is today Rhode Island.

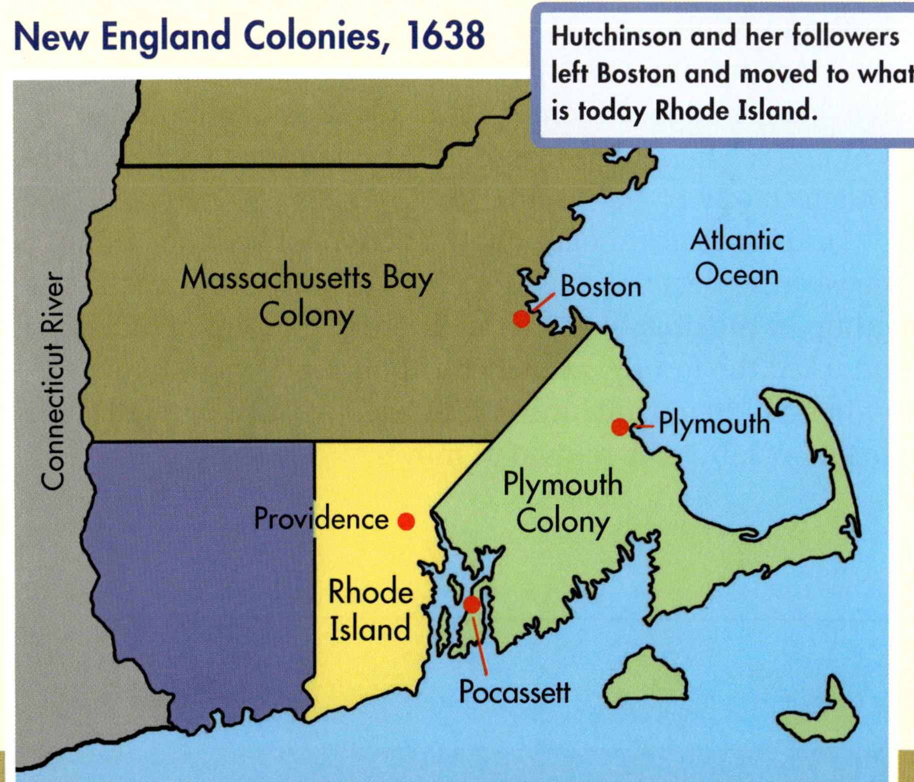

As it turned out, Pocasett was not free from angry debates about religion. Just a year after arriving in Pocasett, the group split in two, and William Coddington led his followers to the southern end of the island. There they founded the town of Newport.

New Amsterdam, in the Dutch colony of New Netherland, became the city of New York.

Hutchinson and her family lived in Pocasett for four years. But in 1642, Hutchinson's husband, William, died. Around this time, Hutchinson heard a rumor that Providence might become part of the Massachusetts Bay Colony. So she and her youngest children moved west to the Dutch colony of New Netherland.

Disaster struck the family the very next year. Relations between settlers and the Mohegan, a Native American group in the area, were tense. In 1643, a group of Mohegan attacked the family and killed Hutchinson and all but one of her children. Hutchinson had been warned by her Dutch neighbors, but she refused to move.

What Anne Hutchinson Left Behind

After the disagreement that ended in Hutchinson's banishment, the ministers agreed that they could never let such opinions split the community again. They decided to set up a college to educate ministers about the true teachings of Puritanism. That college still exists. Today, it is known as Harvard University.

Anne Hutchinson came to the Massachusetts Bay Colony to practice her religion freely. She was highly intelligent and well educated. She spoke up when she disagreed with the ministers and was not afraid to defend her position. Hers was an early voice for the ideas of freedom of conscience and of religion. In the late 1700s, the idea of religious freedom would be guaranteed in the First Amendment of the United States Constitution: "Congress shall make no law respecting an establishment of religion, or prohibiting the free exercise thereof."

A statue of Anne Hutchinson stands in front of the State House in Boston, Massachusetts. It is a tribute to her defense of religious freedom.

Glossary

banish to send away from a place and not allow to return

defendant in a trial, the person who stands accused of a crime

devout having strong religious feeling

official a person in charge of something

persecute to treat unfairly

society a community of people living together who share a system of laws and beliefs